The Greek Re
and its Glo

RODERICK BEATON

The Greek Revolution
of 1821
and its Global
Significance

AIORA

This book is a much-expanded version of an illustrated talk given as part of the British School at Athens Virtual Lecture Series on 12 November 2020. The original talk can be found at https://www.bsa.ac.uk/videos/roderick-beaton-from-the-europe-of-empires-to-the-europe-of-nation-states-the-greek-revolution-of-1821-in-international-context/.

ISBN: 978-618-5369-43-9

First edition July 2021

AIORA PRESS
11 Mavromichali St.
Athens 10679 - Greece
tel: +30 210 3839000
www.aiorabooks.com

CONTENTS

INTRODUCTION

It has been called the 'age of revolution'. The white heat of it came in the decades either side of the year 1800. But it lasted a full century: from the American Declaration of Independence in 1776 to the great national 'unifications' of Germany and Italy during the 1860s, that thereafter would define the geopolitical shape of the European continent and much of the world beyond its shores. Not all of these 'revolutions' were political, or involved violent action or bloodshed. What we call the 'industrial revolution' was just as much a defining development of the age, and set in motion the irreversible shift from reliance on manpower (usually in the form of slaves) to reliance on machines. In the arts, the movement conventionally known as Romanticism has also been called a revolution—a radical (and again, perhaps irreversible) shift in the way that human individuals thought about themselves. It was, according to the philosopher Isaiah Berlin:

> the deepest and most lasting of all changes in the life of the West, no less far-reaching than the three revolutions whose impact is not questioned—the industrial in England, the political in France, and the social and economic in Russia [in 1917].[1]

At one end of this process, the greater part of Europe and its immediate neighbours in western Asia was made up of vast multi-ethnic empires whose possessions stretched across the globe from the Indian subcontinent to the Americas and whose populations nearer home often included several different ethnicities (in today's terms) and speakers of several different languages. At the other, by the 1870s, the stage had been definitively set for the emancipation of subject peoples abroad and the emergence of a new system of politics and governance at home, that of the *nation-state*: according to one

---

[1] Isaiah Berlin, *The Roots of Romanticism* (Princeton, NJ: Princeton University Press, 1999), xiii.

famous definition, based on the idea that 'nations would not be governed by foreigners'.[2] Right in the middle of this long 'age of revolution' and, as it turns out, the pivotal point within it, comes the Greek Revolution that broke out in the spring of 1821.

Historians have been slow to recognise the key role of the Greek uprising in 1821, and the international recognition of Greece as a sovereign, independent state nine years later, in 1830, in this process that did so much to reshape the geopolitics of the European continent, and indeed of much of the world. This little book sets out to explain what happened during these nine years to bring about such far-reaching (and surely unanticipated) consequences, and why the full significance of these events is only now coming to be appreciated, two hundred years later.

---

[2] Lord Acton, cited by Mark Mazower, 'Revolutionary reckonings; Greek independence, 1821 and the historians', *Times Literary Supplement* (26 March 2021), 12.

A GLOBAL STORY

The story begins not in Europe at all, but in the New World. In July 1776, the Declaration of Independence by thirteen British colonies in North America set out the 'self-evident truths' that 'all men are created equal' and enjoy an 'inalienable' right to 'Life, Liberty and the pursuit of Happiness'.[3] The American Revolutionary War ended in 1783, when Great Britain conceded the independence of its former colonies and the United States of America entered the world stage. A new kind of state had been born: a republic whose citizens were in theory sovereign and who voluntarily

---

[3] https://www.archives.gov/founding-docs/declaration-transcript (accessed 13 April 2021).

consented to be governed by a constitution and an executive chosen from among themselves.

The American Revolution was followed not long afterwards by the French, which was sparked by the storming of the Bastille fortress in Paris on 14 July 1789. Under the tripartite slogan, *Liberté, Egalité, Fraternité*, the king, the aristocracy and the Catholic Church were violently overthrown in France during the next few years. As in America, a republic was declared. Former subjects of the crown became 'citizens'; their rights were enshrined in a succession of constitutions. But in France, unlike in America, the revolution had been from the beginning in effect a *civil* war. Instead of battling against a colonial power, different sections of French society were pitted against each other. The excesses of the 'Terror' in 1793 and 1794, when thousands of French people of all classes and both sexes went to the guillotine, shocked the world at the time and have lost little of their horror over the intervening years. The upshot this time was not a viable new republic (at least, not in the short or medium term) but a series of wars that convulsed the whole of Europe, and even reached to the shores of the United States and the islands of the Caribbean, between 1792 and 1815. The attempt by Napoleon Bonaparte, self-proclaimed emperor of France, to conquer the entire continent came to an end with the Battle of Waterloo, fought near Brussels on 18 June 1815.

By that time the European powers, great and small, whose shaky alliances had brought about Napoleon's defeat, had been gathered at Vienna for more than a year to hammer out what became known as the 'Concert of Europe'. This was a set of multilateral understandings designed to ensure that no single state could ever again disturb the peace of the continent as Napoleon had done. The political climate that resulted was as hostile to the kind of changes that had been brought about by the United States and had been attempted by revolutionary France as could be imagined or devised.[4]

But revolutionary zeal, inspired by the American and French examples, was not dead. Its effects were already making themselves felt not in Europe, but once again in the New World. On the island known in Spanish as Hispaniola, in the Caribbean, the French colony of Saint-Domingue had become caught up in the distant revolution in France almost from the beginning,

---

[4] See, for example, Brian Vick, *The Congress of Vienna: Power and Politics after Napoleon* (Cambridge, MA: Harvard University Press, 2014).

The Age of Revolution

1776: American Declaration of Independence

1789: French Revolution

1814–15: Congress of Vienna

1830: Independence of Greece

1848: The Year of Revolutions

1831: Independence of Belgium

1871: Unification of Germany & Unification of Italy

1878: Independence of Serbia, Romania, Montenegro

1908: Independence of Bulgaria

1913: Independence of Albania

1922: Independence of Ireland

1923: Founding of the Republic of Turkey

when Black-African slaves led by Toussaint L'Ouverture proclaimed similar rights for their own people as their white masters were claiming for themselves. In 1804 the colony achieved independence, under its present-day name of Haiti, the first republic after the US to be established in the New World. Then between 1811 and 1825 a series of anti-colonial wars ended colonial rule by Spain and Portugal throughout South America, and established the beginning of the independent republics that make up that continent today. Far beyond the reach of the architects of the 'Concert of Europe', the new type of politics was gaining traction elsewhere.

And despite the best efforts of the new or restored regimes in Europe, there was revolutionary activity in the Old World too. Largely bloodless revolutions by 'constitutionalists' forced significant concessions from monarchs in Spain, in Naples, capital of the Kingdom of the Two Sicilies, in 1820, and in the Alpine kingdom of Piedmont in the spring of 1821. A more general uprising against Austrian rule had been planned in northern Italy for February of that year. But most of these were nipped in the bud. The Spanish constitutionalists lasted the longest, but were crushed by an invasion from France in the spring of 1823.

In 1830, revolutions in Paris in July and in Brussels in August led to significant departures from the settlement that had been laid down at Vienna fifteen years before: a constitutional monarchy, for the first time, in France, and independence for a newly created Kingdom of Belgium the following year. Then the 'year of revolutions' across mainland Europe, in 1848, paved the way for more sweeping and radical changes in the following decades, even though none of these uprisings was successful in itself. The longest surviving of the political architects of the 'Concert of Europe', the Austrian Chancellor Klemens von Metternich, was forced to step aside; the 'Concert' itself, though lip service would continue to be paid to it for more than half a century yet, would never again dominate the continent as it had done until then. After a further series of revolutionary wars and political nation-building, chiefly during the 1860s, the two great 'national unifications' of the nineteenth century, of Germany and Italy, were both formally completed in 1871.

Thereafter, the process gathered pace. In the Balkans, Serbia, Romania and Montenegro gained full independence in 1878, Bulgaria in 1908 and Albania in 1913. The First World War and its aftermath brought an end to the Russian,

Austrian and Ottoman empires, and the creation of further nation-states in eastern Europe and the Middle East, including Turkey in 1923 and Iraq in 1932. The aftermath of World War II, and the process of decolonisation that followed throughout the world, brought many more into existence, on several continents. And the end of the Cold War in 1989 saw the break-up of the Soviet Union and, in the Balkans, of the federal state of Yugoslavia. Yet more nation-states resulted; the most recent of these to gain international recognition being the Republic of Kosovo in 2008. Finally, at the present day, nationalist-separatist movements in many European countries are gaining strength, while tensions rise between nationalist-populist movements on the one hand and the supranational institutions of the European Union (today's equivalent to the 'Concert of Europe'?) on the other. No one can deny that the political process begun by the 'age of revolutions' is alive and active in our own time.

But where, in all this long, and mostly familiar story, is Greece? How does the Greek Revolution of the 1820s fit into the pattern?

Historians of nationalism and national movements, writing in English, have usually been at a loss for how to deal with the Greek Revolution.

Two influential studies, both published in the 1990s, explicitly doubted whether the Greek case was even a national-liberal revolution at all.[5] Others sidestep it rather awkwardly, or treat it as a marginal case. A survey of 'Revolutionary Europe', published in 2020, notes only that in Greece 'nationalism and liberalism came together to produce its own revolutionary moment' —but without really considering how this came about or what its later significance might have been.[6]

Greek historians have a different take, but this too has the effect of isolating the revolution in Greece from events and motivations that were current in many different parts of the world at the same time. Greece was different, the story goes. This way of writing national history is known as 'exceptionalism'. Exceptionalism isn't unique to Greece and Greeks; indeed, *every* nation does it. According to this view, the Greeks had formed a nation since ancient times, and the

---

[5] Eric Hobsbawm, *Nations and Nationalism since 1780: Programme, Myth, Reality* (Cambridge: Cambridge University Press, 1992), 76–7; John Breuilly, *Nationalism and the State* (Manchester: Manchester University Press, 1993), 139–43.

[6] Gavin Murray-Miller, *Revolutionary Europe: Politics, Community and Culture in Transnational Context, 1775–1922* (London: Bloomsbury, 2020), 127.

struggles of the 1820s had been about restoring that nation to its former, rightful condition. At the time and since, Greek independence was regularly referred to as the 'revival', 'regeneration', or even 'resurrection' of *ancient* Greece. Later, during the 1850s and 1860s, the historians Spyridon Zambelios and Konstantinos Paparrigopoulos would refine and extend the narrative to become one, instead, of national 'continuity'—most influentially enshrined in the six-volume *History of the Greek Nation* published by the latter between 1860 and 1877, and perpetuated in authoritative historical works to this day.[7]

But in the context of more than three millennia of Greek history (for which we have evidence through the continued use of the Greek language in both speech and writing), the achievement of national independence wasn't a restoration at all. The Greek nation-state as we know it today, that was created out of the Revolution of the 1820s, is like nothing that had ever existed before, in more

---

[7] Konstantinos Paparrigopoulos, *Ιστορία του ελληνικού έθνους* [*History of the Greek Nation*], 6 vols (Athens, 1860–1877); see most recently the multi-author *Ελληνική ιστορία* (Athens: Ekdotiki Athinon, 2007); see also Roderick Beaton, *Greece: Biography of a Modern Nation* (London: Allen Lane, 2019), 112–14, 129–33.

than three millennia of recorded Greek history. The ancient Greeks, with their fixation on the 'autonomy' of self-governing, mostly small city-states, never managed to make that leap. The Byzantine state, for all its fabled wealth, power and geographical reach, was something else again, and certainly never chose to define itself as 'Hellas' or its people as 'Hellenes', as Greeks have done since 1821. The nation-state that became a reality during the 1820s and 1830s was every bit as much of a novelty for Greeks, even if you accept the argument of Greek exceptionalism, as it was for the rest of the European continent at the time.

This is not to say that the ancient Greeks are irrelevant to the modern story. As we will see, the ancient Greek 'card' would prove to be a trump-card in the hand of the insurgents of the 1820s. But the constant invocation of the 'ancient ancestors', both at the time and ever since, has obscured an essential reality: that Greek sovereign independence was achieved not by ancient, but by modern, Greeks. The Greek revolutionaries and their heirs deserve to be recognised for what they truly were—not a hopelessly belated rearguard to the achievements of their classical predecessors, but as *pioneers* within a much broader, revolutionary movement that was gathering momentum across the world at the time when they rose up against their Ottoman rulers, and to which they were destined to make a key contribution of their own.

Between these two perspectives—the one that treats the Greek case as marginal and of doubtful relevance, the other that detaches it from its nineteenth-century context and creates a new one by connecting it, instead, directly to the ancient world—the true significance of the Greek Revolution has been doubly distorted. The reality is that the Greek Revolution of the 1820s was the first liberal-national movement to succeed in the Old World—*after* the United States, in tandem with similar movements in South America, and *before* all the more familiar national 'unifications' on the continent of Europe. The ideological groundwork had been laid, mostly by thinkers writing in French and German, during the century before. Greeks did not invent the nation-state. But it was in Greece that the experiment was first put into practice in Europe. The outcome of the Greek Revolution turns out to have been the pivotal point on which the whole geopolitical map of Europe tilted, from the eighteenth-century model of multi-ethnic, autocratically ruled empires to the twentieth-century model of the self-determination of nation-states—with consequences for many other parts of the world, too.

How did this come about? What was it about events in Greece, the dynamics and the ideologies of the conflict, that made this outcome possible? The short answer, I believe, is that right from the beginning the Greek uprising was more than a local affair. Broader interests and broader perspectives were involved, as well as the (real) grievances and (once the killing had begun) the urgent need of people on the ground to save their lives and what they could of their livelihoods. From that point of view, it's instructive to compare the Greek revolt with events in Serbia in 1804 and again in 1815. With hindsight, the Serbian uprisings have been claimed as a national struggle too; and it is true that eventually their consequences would morph into one. But even when a degree of autonomy was granted to Serbia in 1817, the conflict had little resonance outside the borders of the Ottoman empire; it changed neither the external frontiers nor, fundamentally, the empire itself. Serbia did not gain full independence until 1878, half a century after Greece. I suggest the reason is that the Serbs fought alone; the Greeks did not.

Let us now consider in more detail the *international dimension* of the Greek Revolution. In

doing so, I do not in the slightest wish to min-
imise the bravery, tactical brilliance, or sheer
determination of the Greeks who fought in the
front line. Their stories have been told many
times, and will doubtless be told many times
again during and after the two hundredth an-
niversary year in 2021. Had it not been for their
actions and their persistence, there could never
have *been* an international dimension. But left
to themselves, might a Theodoros Kolokotronis
or an Odysseus Androutsos have ended up as
another Karageorge of Serbia or Miloš Obrenović,
or like the Princes of Samos from 1834 to 1912
—perhaps lording it over the Peloponnese and
Roumeli respectively, while still formally subject
to the Ottoman sultan? The difference, I suggest,
lies precisely in the international dimension.

FIRST APPEALS TO EUROPE

It began on 6 March 1821 (or 22 February according to the calendar in use in southeastern Europe at the time).[8] A one-armed senior officer in the Russian imperial service slipped across the river Pruth, with a handful of retainers, from what was then Russian territory into Ottoman-

---

[8] The Orthodox Church and the Greek state until March 1923 used the 'old', Gregorian calendar, while all of western Europe had adopted the 'new', Julian calendar by the nineteenth century. 'Old Style' (OS) dates in that century are 12 days earlier than 'New Style' (NS). Histories of the Greek Revolution written in English usually change OS dates to NS, while those written in Greek keep the OS dates that were in use by Greeks at the time. In this book, to avoid confusion, events taking place in Greece and the Ottoman empire are given in double form (OS/NS), while those happening elsewhere in the world are given in their familiar (NS) form only.

controlled Moldavia. Like many high-ranking Russians in those days, his native language was Greek. His name was Alexandros Ypsilantis, and he was the leader of a conspiracy known as the Philiki Etaireia, or Friendly Society. The Society had secretly been recruiting members for a number of years among Greeks of the Ottoman empire and Europe. Two days later, in the Moldavian capital, Jassy (today's Iaşi), Ypsilantis issued a proclamation headed 'Fight for Faith and Fatherland'. It begins:

> The hour has come, o Men of Hellas! [...] The enlightened peoples of Europe, [...] full of gratitude for the benefits bequeathed by our Ancestors to themselves, eagerly await the liberty of the Hellenes.[9]

A month later, in Kalamata, near the southern tip of the Peloponnese, a 'manifesto addressed to Europe by Petros Mavromikhalis, Commander-in-Chief of the Spartan Troops, and the Messenian Senate', announced that the 'unhappy Greeks

---

[9] Ypsilantis's text, dated 24 February [/8 March], is available online at https://el.wikisource.org/wiki/Μάχου_υπέρ_πίστεως _και_πατρίδος (in Greek, my translation, accessed 13 October 2020).

of Peloponnesus' had taken up arms against the 'insupportable yoke of Ottoman tyranny', and went on:

> In this state, deprived of all our rights, we have unanimously resolved to take up arms against our tyrants. [... W]e breathe the air of liberty. Our hands having burst their fetters, already signalize themselves against the barbarians. [...] We invoke therefore the aid of all the civilized nations of Europe, that we may the more promptly attain to the goal of a just and sacred enterprise, reconquer our rights, and regenerate our unfortunate people. Greece, our mother, was the lamp that illuminated you; on this ground she reckons on your active philanthropy.[10]

From the start, the Greek Revolution was never going to be a matter for Greeks alone. Ypsilantis ends by invoking the heroism of the Persian wars, that had been won by the Greek city-states between 490 and 479 BCE, and even calls the Ottomans the 'descendants' of the ancient foe, the Persians. The 'Europe' addressed in these two early appeals is not so much the 'Concert' of

---

[10] Cited in English in Thomas Gordon, *History of the Greek Revolution*, 2 vols (Edinburgh: Blackwood, 1832), 1.183.

ultra-conservative European governments that
actually existed, as the continent that had first
acquired a geopolitical dimension in the pages of
Herodotus, the 'father of history', back in the fifth
century, as he had told the story of the victories
over Persia only a generation afterwards. Exactly as Herodotus had first done, in both these
early documents setting out Greek aims in 1821,
civilised 'Europe' is presented as confronting the
'barbarians' of 'Asia'. This was a perspective that
could be relied on to touch the hearts and minds
of European elites who had been taught at school
that those ancient battles had laid the founda-
tions, not just for the ancient civilisation of the
Greeks, but for all the subsequent history of
the continent too. Only a few decades later, the
British philosopher and imperial civil servant,
John Stuart Mill, could write: 'The battle of
Marathon even as an event in English history is
more important than the battle of Hastings'.[11]

So began a cycle of horrific violence that for a
few months convulsed almost all those parts of
the Ottoman empire where Greeks lived in large

---

[11] John Stuart Mill, 'Grote's *History of Greece I*', in *Essays on
Philosophy and the Classics. Collected Works of John Stuart
Mill*, ed. J.M. Robson (London: Routledge and Kegan Paul,
1978), 271–306 (see 273).

numbers, and in the Aegean and the southern-most tip of the Balkan mainland would drag on for the better part of a decade. During March and April 1821, all of the Danubian principal-ities of Moldavia and Wallachia (today part of Romania), most of what is now mainland Greece, from Thessalonica in the north to the southern Peloponnese, and many towns and islands across the Aegean rose up in response to this call. Noth-ing on such a scale had ever happened before. The Ottomans responded with disproportionate brutality.

In the capital, Constantinople, where a Greek-speaking, Orthodox Christian aristocracy known collectively as the 'Phanariots' had become an indispensible part of the Ottoman state machin-ery, all those Phanariots who had not managed to escape in time were rounded up in reprisal for the behaviour of their compatriots elsewhere, within a few weeks in April and May. Most were publicly beheaded. The seventy-five-year-old Patriarch of the Orthodox Church, Gregory V, was seized at the end of the liturgy on Easter Sunday, 10/22 April, and hanged from the gate of his own precinct. It made no difference that Gregory had been one of those who had publicly condemned the very idea of liberty or revolution, more than a decade before, and only a few weeks previously had excommunicated Ypsilantis and all who responded to his call to arms. Similarly, in Cyprus, where there had been no uprising, the archbishop of the Orthodox Church and leading members of the clergy were put to death anyway, apparently just to set an example. By these extreme measures, the Ottoman state proved effective in restoring or maintaining order throughout most of the Greek-speaking world that lay within its dominions.

But in the southern part of the Greek mainland—in the Peloponnese, in parts of what was then known as Roumeli further north, and on several islands of the Aegean—the revolt had taken hold and there was no stopping it. Local leaders, backed by former brigands and irregular bands of their armed followers, seized the initiative and swept across the country. By the end of 1821, the countryside throughout the Peloponnese and southern Roumeli had been subjected to what today would be termed 'ethnic cleansing'. Those Muslims who had not fled, been killed or, in a few high-ranking cases, ransomed, had taken refuge in a string of fortresses that went back to Crusader or Byzantine times. The decisive victory of the first year of the war was the submission of the fortified town of Tripolitsa, the capital of the Morea, in early October. After the town capitulated, some eight thousand Muslim and Jewish inhabitants were slaughtered.

On the ground, and among the rank and file who had the most to lose, the conflict that had begun was a war of religion. In the language of the time, all Muslims were described as 'Turks', irrespective of what today would be called their ethnicity. Many of those killed at Tripolitsa, including probably all of the Jews, will have spoken Greek as their first language, most of the Muslims either Greek or Albanian. It was religion that determined who was to live and who to die. And from this time on, no quarter was given by either side.

The aftermath of the taking of Tripolitsa would seriously damage the image of the Revolution abroad. But it was soon followed by even greater savagery shown by the Ottomans to the Greek inhabitants of the island of Chios during the spring and summer of 1822. The Greeks of Chios had resolutely refused to have anything to do with the Greek insurgency elsewhere. Their farmers, traders and ship's captains had grown rich on the rare crop of mastic, a form of chewing gum much in demand among the ladies of the harem in Istanbul, and thought to have medicinal properties. But on 10/22 March of that year, a small fleet of Greek ships from the island of Samos, to the south, landed fifteen hundred armed men on the coast of Chios. They were easily able to take control of the island. The Turkish garrison was outnumbered, and fled to the safety of the citadel above the main town. Chios was proclaimed part of free Greece. That meant not just a major loss to the Ottoman state, so close to its Anatolian heartland and the capital, Istanbul. It also meant no more mastic for the ladies of the harem to chew.

The Sultan reacted with a deadly escalation. Three weeks after the Greeks had landed, the Ottoman fleet under its admiral, Kara Ali, dis-embarked a force of fifteen thousand soldiers on Chios. It was the beginning of one of the most horrific massacres of a horrible war. The Samians who had started it all could make their escape in their ships. But there was no defence for the Greeks of Chios, most of whom had taken no part in the action. By the time the killing was over, the trees that produced the precious mastic crop had gone the same way as the growers. It would be a generation before the supply of mastic to Istanbul could be restored to anything like its previous levels. The thirst for vengeance had cut off the highest levels of Ottoman society from one of their staple luxuries. Of the 100,000 Greeks who had lived in Chios before the massacres, it is said

Massacres of Chios after Eugène Delacroix. Lithograph.
Koraes Library, Chios.

that by the end of the summer of 1822 only 30,000
were left. The rest had been killed, sold as slaves,
or escaped to islands under Greek control.[12]

---

[12] Gordon, *History*, 1.357–68.

The shockwaves of these massacres spread all over Europe. There was a hardheaded financial aspect to this reaction. European banks and businesses had been heavily invested in the once-prosperous ship-owners of Chios. Now some of them were exposed to huge losses. But by far the greatest response was what we would nowadays call humanitarian. A painting on the subject by Eugène Delacroix was exhibited in Paris two years after the events, in 1824. Standing more than twelve feet high, it captures on an epic scale the sense of horror that had swept through the continent. The full title of the painting is 'Scenes of massacres at Chios; Greek families awaiting death or slavery, etc.'

The French poet and novelist, Victor Hugo, best known for the novel *Les Misérables*, picked out the detail of a boy clutching at his dead mother's breast in a poem that he wrote not long after seeing it:

The Turks have been here. All is ruin and
  mourning.
Chios, the island of wines, is nothing but a
  sombre reef. [...]
What do you want? flower, beautiful fruit, or
  the marvellous bird?
—Friend, said the Greek child, said the child

with blue eyes,
I want gunpowder and bullets.[13]

Even the British Foreign Secretary, Lord Castlereagh, a staunch supporter of Metternich and the 'Concert of Europe' and an enemy of revolutions everywhere, was moved to outrage. An official protest to the Ottoman government followed.[14] The plight of Christians in the face of Muslim 'barbarity' was beginning to resonate around Europe and as far away as the United States of America. It would be some time yet before foreign governments were ready to take a hand. But the extreme and disproportionate violence meted out to their Christian subjects by the Ottomans was one of the first factors that began to move political leaders abroad in that direction.

---

[13] Gary Bass, *Freedom's Battle: The Origins of Humanitarian Intervention* (New York: Vintage, 2009), 73.

[14] Douglas Dakin, *The Greek Struggle for Independence, 1821–1833* (London: Batsford, 1973), 148–50.

CONTESTED MEANINGS
OF LIBERTY

In the meantime, at the end of 1821, in Greece a first 'national assembly' had brought together representatives from all the areas that had been liberated, to draw up a constitution. The site chosen, in the north-eastern Peloponnese, lay close to the remains of the ancient theatre and sanctuary of the healing god Asclepius at Epidaurus. The first provisional constitution that emerged has ever since been known as the Epidaurus Constitution. Among its opening provisions are these, that define the state and its citizens:

> All indigenous inhabitants of the Land of Greece (Hellas) who believe in Christ are Hellenes and are entitled to an equal enjoyment of every right.

All Greeks are equal before the laws without any exception, whether of rank, or class, or office.[15]

It has been noted that these articles place equality above liberty 'in the hierarchy of values of the Greek people', and that this 'has become a steadfast characteristic of all Greek constitutions' subsequently.[16] But of even greater significance was the decision, for the first time formalised, that the new political state was to be known by the ancient name of 'Hellas', and its citizens as 'Hellenes'. So effective has that collective act of re-invention been that it requires an effort of imagination, today, to realise how innovative it was at the time. Many Greeks would still continue to think of themselves as 'Romans' (*Romioi*), in everyday contexts and informally among themselves, for at least a century and a half after that. But the *official* designations, revived

---

[15] Provisional Constitution of Greece, 1[/13] January 1822, p. 2: section II, articles 2 and 3 (my translation), available online at https://www.hellenicparliament.gr/UserFiles/f3c70a23-7696-49db-9148-f24dce6a27c8/syn06.pdf (accessed 13 April 2021).

[16] Nicos Alivizatos, 'Assemblies and constitutions', in Paschalis Kitromilides and Constantinos Tsoukalas (eds), *The Greek Revolution: A Critical Dictionary* (Cambridge, MA: Harvard University Press, 2021), 439–52 (444 cited).

The official stamps of the Executive Corps and the Legislative Corps, 1823. National Historical Museum, Athens.

from the ancient world and adapted to the new political reality that was then being shaped, have never since been questioned.

Other elements of this first constitution would turn out to be casualties of the actual process of gaining independence. Republican government was one of these. Others were elements drawn from the republican constitutions of revolutionary France. The separation of powers between an 'Executive Corps' and a 'Legislative Corps' partly drew on the same sources, but also enshrined an essential element of the US Constitution, that remains an essential article of many democratic systems around the world today. In the event it would take many decades for independent Greece to achieve all these aims of its first founders. But the *aspirations* are clearly set out in this early document of 1822. And even if many of these were designed as much

for foreign consumption as to be practically im-
plemented at home, the gesture itself would
prove to be enormously important and to have
consequences. Such major figures abroad as the
English political philosopher Jeremy Bentham
and the former president of the USA, Thomas
Jefferson, were induced to enter into debate
on its provisions. Even if so far only on paper,
Greece was already on the way to becoming a
modern state, run on the most forward-looking
constitutional principles of the time.

In practice, however, and on the ground, the
leaders of the Revolution were soon at logger-
heads over which course to pursue. For the
architects of the Epidaurus Constitution, and
the modified versions that would follow during
the next few years, the key to ultimate success
would lie in drawing foreign powers into the
conflict, essentially in internationalising their
struggle. But many of those who had done the
most to liberate their local areas by force of
arms were reluctant to see the gains they had
made slip into the hands of outsiders—meaning
equally Greeks from places further afield, such
as Constantinople or the Greek-ruled principalities of Wallachia and Moldavia, and foreigners.
It is often said that every revolution brings in

its train a civil war; the Greek Revolution was no exception. Civil war broke out twice during 1824, in the spring and summer and then again more briefly in December. At issue was the meaning of the freedom that had been won, and the future direction of the lands and communities that were now struggling to manage their own affairs, at the same time as fighting to hold off Ottoman counter-attacks on several fronts.

On one side were those whom historians today call 'modernisers', 'centralisers', or 'constitutionalists'. Most prominent and influential among them during the early years of the conflict was Alexandros Mavrokordatos. Born in Constantinople in 1791, into one of the most influential of all the Phanariot families of the previous century, Mavrokordatos was one of the few men in revolutionary Greece to sport a western European frock-coat. He cut an unheroic figure, standing not much more than five feet tall, stout, and wearing thick-lensed spectacles for his myopia. But Mavrokordatos was a consummate politician, master of eight languages, committed to the humanitarian and secular ideas of the European Enlightenment and deeply versed in the political theory and geopolitics of the day. He had been primarily responsible for the final draft of the Epidaurus Constitution, had successfully steered its provisions through the assembly, and then been rewarded by being elected president of the Executive Corps—in effect president of revolutionary Greece—for a one-year term in 1822.

On the other side were the warlords, the men who had been much the most effective in fighting the Revolution's early battles. For them, 'liberty' meant absolute self-sufficiency and a corresponding refusal to acknowledge any authority other than their own. Among their ranks, the leader was the strongest and the most charismatic, and the leader's word was law. Their power bases were local, or at most regional. They had no great interest in widening the conflict, still less in encouraging foreign intervention—though they tended, not entirely consistently, to make an exception for Russia, the only foreign power that shared the Orthodox religion that united the Greek revolutionaries. The most powerful among the warlords in the Peloponnese was Theodoros Kolokotronis, a former brigand and paid soldier of successive foreign governments in the Ionian islands. Nicknamed 'the Old Man of the Morea' (he was fifty years old when the revolution began), Kolokotronis was a formidable guerrilla chieftain. By the second year of the revolution he had a string of victories to his credit. Among

Theodoros Kolokotronis at the Castle of Damala (Troezen)
and *Alexandros Mavrokordatos at Poros.*
Drawings by Karl Krazeisen, 1827. National Gallery, Athens.

them was the annihilation of an Ottoman army
that had tried and failed to relieve the besieged
garrison in Nafplio and had then been trapped
by Kolokotronis's men in the narrow pass of
Dervenakia, near Corinth, in June 1822.

These opposing mentalities can be captured
in their purest, most extreme form, in the
stand-off that took place in the summer of
1823 between the two men. On 12/24 July, in
Tripolitsa, Kolokotronis, who at the time had
been elected Vice-President of the Executive,
summoned the president-elect of the Legislative
Corps (Mavrokordatos) and told him that
unless he resigned his office at once he would
mount him backwards on a donkey and have

him chased out of the Peloponnese with whips
—or as Kolokotronis himself much later re-
called: 'I'll come and chase you out with lemons,
in the same frock-coat you came with.'[17] So
much for the principle of the separation of powers. Mavrokordatos and the parliamentarians
fled the Peloponnese, leaving the field tem-
porarily to Kolokotronis and the warlords. By
the end of 1823 Greece had two governments,
one based in the village of Kranidi in the north-
east Peloponnese and made up of modernisers
and their sympathisers, and a rival dominated
by Kolokotronis and Petrobey Mavromichalis
in Tripolitsa. During the next year, supporters
of each would fight it out in open civil war.[18]

Part of what was at stake was the very issue
of whether to internationalise their struggle
with continuing appeals to foreigners for military, financial and diplomatic support, or to go
it alone. What had immediately roused the ire
of Kolokotronis, on that July day in Tripolitsa,

---

[17] See, respectively, Roderick Beaton, *Byron's War: Romantic
Rebellion, Greek Revolution* (Cambridge: Cambridge Univer-
sity Press, 2013), 157 (citing an unpublished report, in
English, sent to Byron on 13 September 1823); Theodoros
Kolokotronis, Απομνημονεύματα [Memoirs], transcribed G.
Tertsetis, ed. T. Vournas, Athens: Drakopoulos, n.d.), 136.

[18] Beaton, *Byron's War*, 147–57; Beaton, Greece, 85–90.

was the discovery that Mavrokordatos had despatched the first of a series of appeals to the British Foreign Secretary, George Canning, asking for support for the revolution in Greece. In them, Mavrokordatos argued, cogently and at some length, that the Ottoman empire was on its last legs. As Ottoman power weakened in eastern Europe and the eastern Mediterranean, the resulting power vacuum would be filled by Russia, to the detriment of western states, especially Britain and France. This was the diplomatic dilemma that would shortly become known as the Eastern Question, and would not finally be resolved until after the First World War. The answer, according to Mavrokordatos, was for the western European powers to support a strong and independent Greece as a counter-weight to Russia.

Shortly afterwards, the provisional government despatched commissioners (again on the initiative of Mavrokordatos) to London to try to raise a loan from private speculators. This policy, too, lay at the heart of the 'modernising' project—though it would prove to have fateful consequences for the future Greek state, from its first insolvency crisis in 1827 to its latest, in the 2010s. Of this, too, Kolokotronis and those who thought like him were deeply suspicious.

Explaining himself through an interpreter to
emissaries sent by Lord Byron, in September
1823, long before he dictated his more famous
Memoirs, the 'Old Man of the Morea' expressed
his objection like this:

> because Great Britain might thereby obtain an
> undue preponderance in Greece, which country
> he wished to be entirely unfettered, and that it
> might tend to aid the intrigues of Mavrocordato
> and the Phanariots, who [...] would contrive to
> appropriate to themselves the lion's share of it
> [the loan].[19]

Victory in the civil wars of 1824 went to
the modernisers. By the start of the next year,
Greece was on course to become a western-
style, centralised state on the newly emerging
national model. But both the conflict and the
character of the protagonists in that internal
struggle have left a profound legacy that is still
with us to this day. At the time, and ever since,
the 'Old Man of the Morea' has cut a charis-

---

[19] Beaton, *Byron's War*, 152–3, citing James Hamilton Browne,
'Narrative of a visit, in 1823, to the seat of war in Greece',
Blackwood's Edinburgh Magazine, vol. 36, no. 226 (Septem-
ber 1834), 392-407 (404 quoted).

matic figure in the imagination of Greeks, while *political* architects of the state, such as Mavrokordatos, have languished out of sight. According to an opinion poll carried out in Greece in December 2019, 92.7 per cent of respondents named Kolokotronis among the most important leaders of the Revolution, with a lead of almost 30 per cent over his nearest rival, while Mavrokordatos polled a mere 3.7 per cent.[20] The internal split that came to the surface back then has never entirely gone away since, and would re-surface as a fault-line in many different later crises in Greek history.

---

[20] *Πώς βλέπουν οι Έλληνες την Επανάσταση του 1821: ανάλυση* [*How Do Greeks See the Revolution of 1821: Analysis*] (Athens: Kefim, 2020), 15.

IMPACT ABROAD

By the time that the internal conflict was resolved at the end of 1824, events in Greece were beginning to generate an impact abroad that went far beyond public outrage at atrocities committed against fellow-Christians. The first appeals to European governments by the Greek revolutionaries had fallen on predictably deaf ears. Tsar Alexander had very publicly denounced the actions of Ypsilantis in the Danubian principalities, and had stripped him of all his Russian ranks and titles, while attending one of the periodic congresses of European leaders, called to reinforce the 'Concert of Europe', in March 1821. A year and a half later, a Greek delegation was barred from even attending another (the last of these congresses, as it would turn out) held at

Verona between October and December 1822. Only from the tiny breakaway republic of Haiti came a profession of political support, in the form of a letter written by its president, Jean-Pierre Boyer, on 15 January 1822:

> With great enthusiasm we learned that Hellas was finally forced to take up arms in order to gain her freedom and the position that she once held among the nations of the world. Such a beautiful and just cause and, most importantly, the first successes which have accompanied it, cannot leave Haitians indifferent, for we, like the Hellenes, were for long subjected to a dishonourable slavery and finally, with our own chains, broke the head of tyranny.[21]

In Europe, every government still shunned the insurgents. But the same could not be said

---

[21] Ioannis Philemon, Δοκίμιον ιστορικόν περί της Ελληνικής Επαναστάσεως [Historical Essay concerning the Greek Revolution], 4 vols (Athens: Karyofyllis, 1859–61), 4.368-9 (letter from the President of Haiti to A. Koraes and three other prominent Greeks in Paris, cited in Greek translation), trans. E.G. Sideris and A.A. Konsta, 'A letter from Jean-Pierre Boyer to Greek revolutionaries', Journal of Haitian Studies 11/1 (2005), 167–71 (168 cited). I am grateful to Dr Georgios Giannakopoulos for bringing this source to my attention.

for individuals and pressure groups in many countries. Volunteers came from every corner of the European continent, and from as far away as America. They were known as 'philhellenes' (lovers of things Greek). This was the first time, possibly in the whole of world history, that so many individuals from so many different countries and backgrounds left their homes to fight in somebody else's war, without anyone else compelling them to do it, or (in almost all cases) without any mercenary expectation of financial gain. Indeed, especially in the first years, the authorities in their countries of origin took rigorous steps to prevent them from leaving, fearing what today would be called the spread of 'radicalization'. It has sometimes been suggested that these volunteers, and their far more numerous supporters back home, were the pioneers of the later phenomenon of humanitarian intervention. But the truth is that they went to Greece to fight for something that they believed was their own, something in which they believed that their own societies and governments ought to have no less of a stake.[22]

---

[22] William St Clair, *That Greece Might Still Be Free: The Philhellenes in the War of Independence* (London: Open Book, 2008; first published 1972); Roderick Beaton, 'Philhellenism', in

To appreciate what this was, we have to re-member that in Europe and America, the 'Greek Revival' in public architecture was at its height during the first decades of the nineteenth century. This was the time when the citizens of Edinburgh, for example, began to promote their city as the 'new Athens' or the 'Athens of the North'; a replica of the Parthenon was designed to crown the Calton Hill near the city centre, and the foundation stone was actually laid in the same year as the Greek Revolution began (though unlike the revolution in Greece, that project would soon be abandoned, to leave the single row of columns that can be seen on the Edinburgh skyline today). The Royal High School was built to an ancient Greek design, as was St Pancras New Church on the Euston Road in London, built between 1819 and 1822, with its Caryatid porch exactly mimicking the Erechtheion on the Acropolis of Athens. More than ever before, painters, architects, histori-ans, poets, and political thinkers in Britain, continental Europe and the United States were drawing inspiration from classical Greece, and

---

Kitromilides and Tsoukalas (eds), *The Greek Revolution*, 593–613. On humanitarian intervention see Bass, *Freedom's Battle*, 51–151.

particularly from the achievements of Athens in the fifth century BCE. It had been there, after all, that the idea of democratic self-government had first been born; revolutionary constitutions everywhere, in the early nineteenth century, paid tribute to the ancient precedents of democratic Athens, as well as of republican Rome.

Well before the revolution had broken out in 1821, the twenty-one-year-old Lord Byron had embarked on his 'Grand Tour' in Greek lands in 1809. Three years later he had gone on to publish the first two cantos of *Childe Harold's Pilgrimage*. In that poem he had speculated about the possibility that the 'children' of the ancient Greeks might rise up and abolish their 'bondage' to the Ottoman Turks:

Fair Greece! Sad relic of departed worth!
Immortal though no more; though fallen, great!
Who now shall lead thy scattered children forth,
And long accustomed bondage uncreate?[23]

Byron's poem had become a runaway bestseller when it first appeared in 1812 and before

---

[23] Lord Byron, *Childe Harold's Pilgrimage*, canto 2, lines 693–7, in Jerome McGann (ed.), *Lord Byron, The Major Works* (Oxford: Oxford University Press, 2000), 75.

long had been translated into most of the languages of Europe. At the same time as Byron was becoming an international celebrity, so were Greece and the Greeks that he wrote about.

To Byron's friend and fellow-poet, Percy Bysshe Shelley, it was self-evident, once the revolution had begun in Greece in 1821, that 'Our laws, our literature, our religion, our arts have their root in Greece'. For this reason, Shelley argued, in the preface to his poem *Hellas*, published early the next year, 'We are all Greeks'.[24] It was this sense of a shared heritage that brought the philhellenes to make common cause with a foreign people of whom they knew almost nothing, in a land that very few of them had ever visited.

Of those who went to Greece as volunteers, by far the most famous was Byron himself, whose practical contribution to strengthening the political hand of Mavrokordatos and the legitimate provisional government in facing down the warlords was tragically cut short by his death from fever, at Missolonghi, on 7/19 April 1824. Among others were two of the earliest and still most authoritative historians of the Revolution,

---

[24] 'Preface' to Hellas, in *The Complete Poetical Works of Percy Bysshe Shelley*, ed. Thomas Hutchinson (London: Oxford University Press, 1943), 446–8 (447 cited).

Lord Byron.
Drawing by P. Stavropoulos,
after the painting
by Richard Westall.

Thomas Gordon and George Finlay, both them Scots.[25] As a military force, despite the aura of fame that surrounds many individual names, the philhellenes contributed almost nothing to the successful outcome of the Revolution. Their total number was probably no more than twelve hundred. Almost a third of those lost their lives, either in combat or, like Byron, from disease.[26] They won no significant victories. None of the attempts that they spearheaded, to build up the regular armed forces necessary to establish and maintain a functioning modern state, was successful during the Revolution. The creation of a Greek national army would have to wait until the

---

[25] Gordon, *History*; George Finlay, *History of the Greek Revolution*, 2 vols (Edinburgh: Blackwood, 1861).

[26] St Clair, *That Greece*, 355–6.

1830s, after independence had been won. It was not on the battlefield that the most important contribution of the philhellenes lay, but far behind the lines, in the countries from which those volunteers had set out.

During the 1820s, philhellenic initiatives sprang up spontaneously in most parts of Europe, and in the USA. Activity took a wide variety of forms: setting up voluntary committees and fundraising, reporting and commentary in the press, reflections of philhellenic themes in the arts, even (latterly) large-scale fundraising for the cause and lobbying governments at home. The scale of participation is impossible even to estimate. But clearly it was of a magnitude that far outweighed the limited numbers who went to Greece with the expectation that they would join in the struggle there. With justice, the philhellenism 'of the home front' has been characterised as a Europe-wide 'movement' that mobilised many thousands of individuals and diverse communities, across national and state borders. 'To be a philhellene,' in the words of the French scholar Denys Barau, 'was to wish to participate in history in the making'.[27]

---

[27] Denys Barau, *La Cause des Grecs, une histoire du mouvement philhellène (1821–1829)* (Paris: Honoré Champion, 2009),

GRAND CONCERT

EN FAVEUR

DES GRECS.

PREMIÈRE PARTIE.

1. Ouverture d'Olympia, de Spontini.
2. Air chanté par Mᵐᵉ L***, amateur.
3. Fantaisie de Flûte, de M. Lahou, exécutée par un amateur.
4. *Della Tromba*, air de Puccitta, chanté par Mᵐᵉ T***, amateur.
5. Chœur des Bardes, musique de Lesueur.

SECONDE PARTIE.

1. Ouverture d'Évelina, de Rossini.
2. *La Gloria*, air de Paer, chanté par Mᵐᵉ T***, amateur.
3. Symphonie de Beethoven.
4. Air varié pour la Clarinette, exécuté par un amateur.
5. Missolunghi, scène lyrique, paroles de M. L***, musique de M. Hanssens, jeune.

Le Concert commencera à six heures.

Bruxelles, 3 juin 1826.

IMPRIMERIE DE C. J. DE MAT FILS ET H. REMY,
RUE DES GRANDS CARMES.

Concert in Brussels, in 1826, in support of the Greek Revolution. Collection of the Society for Hellenism and Philhellenism and the Philhellenism Museum, Athens.

It was very much as a result of these activities that governments abroad slowly, and usually reluctantly, began to reassess their position

---

25, 713, the latter cited; on the significance of the 'home front', see 321–96.

towards Greece. Great Britain was the first to break ranks among the 'Concert of Europe'. Early in 1823, George Canning, who had recently been appointed Foreign Secretary, recognised the captains and crews of Greek ships on the high seas as legitimate belligerents (rather than as pirates). At the end of the same year, in the USA, President James Monroe came close to recognising Greek independence in a famous speech to Congress. Mainly remembered for setting out the 'Monroe Doctrine', which defined respective spheres of influence for Europe and the New World, the presidential address of 2 December also included these words: 'There is good cause to believe [...] that Greece will become again an independent nation. That she may obtain that rank is the object of our most ardent wishes'. A little over a year later, a bill was introduced to Congress that would have explicitly recognised Greek independence. Even though it failed, public support in America remained strong enough to allow the fighting frigate *Hellas* to be built in a New York shipyard and delivered to the Greek government at the end of 1826.[28]

---

[28] Bass, *Freedom's Battle*, 91–7 (95 cited).

In Europe, no government was yet prepared to go so far. In 1824, Tsar Alexander secretly sounded out the British and French about carving out 'zones of influence' for each of them in an autonomous Greece which would still be nominally subject to the Ottomans. When the tsar's proposal was leaked, the Greeks saw this as a betrayal. A year later, in a rare moment of unanimity, the leaders of the provisional government and the most powerful warlords came together to address a plea to London, in which they declared, 'the Greek nation places the sacred deposit of its liberty, independence, and political existence, under the absolute protection of Great Britain'.[29] Although the British government refused, and while different factions in Greece put out alternative feelers to both France and Russia, a diplomatic dialogue had begun. Greece was firmly on the agenda of the chief maritime powers of the day.

---

[29] Gordon, *History*, 2.283–4.

THE GREAT POWERS
TAKE A HAND

From the point of view of the Greeks, it was not a moment too soon. By the time that plea was issued, on 20 July/1 August 1825, the Ottoman counter-attack had begun. In spring 1825, Ottoman land forces struck down from the north while a newly modernised fleet from Alexandria, commanded by Ibrahim Pasha, the son of the sultan's vassal, Muhammad Ali of Egypt, landed troops on the south coast of the Peloponnese. Within a few months Ibrahim had retaken all the Greeks' gains south of the Isthmus of Corinth except Nafplio, the capital, which held out. Farther north, in Roumeli, only two towns remained in Greek hands: Missolonghi in the west and Athens in the east. The first fell after a year-long siege in April 1826, the second in May the next year, after a series of costly attempts to relieve the besieged garrison on the Acropolis.

By the summer of 1827 the Greek situation was desperate. But too many Greeks had struggled for too long to think of going back now. The ferocity of Ottoman reprisals was all too well known, by this time. There would be nothing to be gained by submission. Ibrahim, who had been promised the Peloponnese as his reward, was threatening to kill or enslave the remaining population and people the entire region with Muslims transported from North Africa. It was not only Greeks who were galvanised by these threats. Philhellenes had been mobilised throughout the world. It was becoming impossible any longer for their governments to ignore them.

From the spring of 1826, the three Great Powers that had interests in the eastern Mediterranean—Great Britain, France and Russia—embarked on a delicate series of negotiations, not with the Greeks, but with each other. If Ottoman power was going to be seriously weakened in Europe, as Mavrokordatos had prophesied in his letters to the British Foreign Secretary, it mattered a great deal to each of the three that neither of the others should gain a geopolitical advantage from the outcome: the 'Eastern Question' again. In 1827, the three powers agreed to send a joint naval taskforce into the Aegean, charged with enforcing a truce between the belligerents.

Not surprisingly, the Greeks welcomed this sign of military intervention. The Ottoman authorities, from the sultan downwards, had consistently maintained that the rebellion by some of his Christian subjects was a purely internal matter for the empire to deal with as it saw fit; no foreign power had the right to try to intervene. And so the stage was set for one of the few great set-piece battles of the entire war. Instead of imposing peace, the squadrons of the three allied navies ended up engaging the combined fleets of the sultan and of his Egyptian vassal in Navarino Bay, off the southwest coast of the Peloponnese, on 8/20 October 1827. The Ottoman and Egyptian fleets were all but destroyed, and Ibrahım was forced to abandon the Peloponnese shortly afterwards.

The success of the Greek Revolution, in some form, was now assured. But the eventual settlement had been taken out of Greek hands. It was now up to the three Great Powers to find a resolution. This would not materialise immediately, however. In the meantime, it was the provisional government of Greece, and not any external

Battle of Navarino. Engraving by Robert William Smart and
Henry Pyall, after drawings by Sir John Theophilus Lee,
circa 1830. National Historical Museum, Athens.

agent, that appointed an interim head of government for the state that still had no formally recognized existence. His name was Ioannis Kapodistrias, also known as Count John Capo d'Istria. Originally an aristocrat from Corfu, he had joined the Russian service and risen to become joint foreign minister of Russia from 1814 to 1822. Kapodistrias arrived in the Peloponnese early in 1828, with the title *Kyvernitis*, which exactly translates the Latin-derived term 'governor'.

Kapodistrias was at once an outsider—he had never been to mainland Greece before—and a Greek. His appointment was accepted by the representatives of the Great Powers who were now in charge of the negotiations for Greece's future, though for different reasons he was distrusted by the governments of all three. But at least, from their point of view, they were dealing with a statesman whose credentials were widely recognized—Kapodistrias had after all helped to represent Russia at the Congress of Vienna. His arrival was another significant step towards the emergence of Greece onto the European stage.

The new Governor at once set about establishing the institutions of the future nation-state. He established a system of education and encouraged the founding of new schools using the latest experimental methods from Britain and continental Europe. He introduced Greece's first modern currency, based on a coin called the phoenix, and an embryonic national bank. He organized the judiciary. He began work on a much-needed land registry—which remains much-needed and incomplete, almost two centuries later. He also introduced that staple of every Greek *taverna* and restaurant in later times, the potato.

On the diplomatic front, Kapodistrias did his best to negotiate the most favourable terms for Greece with the representatives of the three Great Powers. Although international treaties had begun to refer to 'Greece', since April 1826, as some kind of a political entity, none of the diplomatic exchanges so far had envisaged anything more radical than a degree of 'autonomy' within the bounds of the Ottoman empire. Nominally, at least, the liberated Greeks would continue to count as subjects of the sultan. Kapodistrias did everything he could to change this, and to push for complete independence. But, ironically enough, the decisive breakthrough was achieved, not by a Greek initiative, but the defeat of the Ottoman empire by Russia in yet another Russo-Turkish war in September 1829.

This war had begun the previous year, and had been fought mainly in the Caucasus; the future of the Greeks had not been its main cause. But when Russian troops came as close to the Ottoman capital as Edirne (Adrianople), even the Duke of Wellington, at the time prime minister of Great Britain, and no friend to revolutions in general or to the Greeks in particular, suddenly saw the force of the argument that had first been put by Mavrokordatos to Canning, back in 1823. 'We must reconstruct a Greek Empire,' Wellington wrote to his Foreign Secretary, Lord Aberdeen; 'no Power of Europe ought to take anything for itself excepting the Emperor of Russia a sum for his expenses.'[30] After this, it was the British government, grudgingly, and motivated by distrust of its allies, that threw the final, unlooked-for ingredient into the mix. Now, asked Wellington, why should not this new Greece be fully independent? That way, all three powers, as well as the Ottoman empire, would be obliged to give up any pretension they may have had to rule Greece as their own dependency.

And so it happened that on 3 February 1830, not on the battlefield or even in Greece at all, but in a dry conclave of dignitaries held at the British Foreign Office on Whitehall, Greece for the first

---

[30] Dakin, *The Greek Struggle for Independence*, 273 (letter dated 11 September 1829).

time became fully sovereign and independent. Present were the British Foreign Secretary, Lord Aberdeen, and the ambassadors of France and Russia. According to a diplomatic protocol signed by the three, 'Greece will form an independent State, and will enjoy all those rights—political, administrative, and commercial—attached to complete independence'.[31] Greece (or Hellas / Ellada in Greek) was born at that moment and took its place on the political map of Europe. The Revolution was not yet over—because it would take another two years for all the details to be worked out, including frontiers and the system of government. But that date in February 1830 marks the turning point.

---

[31] Ministry of Foreign Affairs of Greece, Service of Historical Archives, *The Foundation of the Modern Greek State: Major Treaties and Conventions (1830–1947)*, ed. Ph. Constantopoulou (Athens: Kastaniotis, 1999), 30 (in French); facsimile of the original in J.M. Wagstaff, *Greece: Ethnicity and Sovereignty, 1820–1994. Atlas and Documents* (Archive Editions) [Cambridge: Cambridge University Press], 2002, 141–5.

ENDGAME

A year and a half later, back in Greece, Kapodistrias was assassinated. The cause was the latest
in the series of far-reaching domestic reforms
that he had imposed on his countrymen. This
was a unified, national system of taxation. The
tough, independent-minded highlanders of Mani,
the southernmost part of the Peloponnese, had
never paid taxes to the Ottomans. Petrobey
Mavromichalis and his clansmen saw no reason
why they should be compelled to do so now,
when they had just won their liberty. The tax revolt in the Mani was put down by force. Petrobey
and several of his relatives were imprisoned,
effectively held as hostages, in Nafplio. But the
honour of the clan had been slighted. Despite
being under armed guard, the brother and son of

The assassination of I. Kapodistrias. Lithograph by an unknown artist. National Historical Museum, Athens.

Petrobey, Konstantinos and Georgios, gunned down the Governor on the morning of Sunday, 27 September / 9 October 1831, as he was entering church in Nafplio. For several months after that, Greece was plunged into a third round of civil war, as warlords and their supporters refused to concede any power or influence to their rivals.

This was the background to the endgame of the Revolution, which once again was played out far from Greece. It had taken some time for the three Great Powers to follow through after the London Protocol of 1830. Upheavals in France, Belgium, Poland, and a change of government in Great Britain, had already drawn attention away from Greece, even before the assassination. By this time it had already been decided that the new state must be a monarchy, not a republic as had been envisaged by several successive provisional constitutions. In May 1832, a new treaty determined that Prince Otto, the second son of the philhellene King of Bavaria, Ludwig I, would be the first king. Frontiers for the kingdom were drawn up at the same time. They included only the Peloponnese, less than half of mainland Greece as it is today, and those islands closest to it in the Aegean. The remainder was still part of the Ottoman empire, except for the Ionian

Otto, Royal Prince of Bavaria, 1831, Johann Heinrich Richter.
University and State Library of Darmstadt.

islands, which had been awarded to Great Britain to rule as a protectorate in 1815. Neither the Greeks nor the Ottomans had any say in these decisions (though the sultan did sign a treaty with the European powers, on 22 July the same year, recognising the independence and the frontiers of Greece).[32]

At the time and for long afterwards, even today, many Greeks have felt sore at this outcome. What had been won fell some way short of the absolute ideal of 'Liberty or Death' that so many had fought and died for. And it is true that new foreign debts, incurred at the time of independence, and sometimes the blatant interference of the 'protector' powers until well into the twentieth century, would severely curtail the sovereignty that had been promised by the founding treaties. On the other hand, the Revolution had begun with appeals from its leaders to the peoples and governments of Europe for support. Had it not been for the determination of the Greek people to fight on, in the face of massacres and mass enslavement, and against overwhelming odds, the Revolution could not have succeeded as it did. That achievement belongs

---

[32] Wagstaff, *Greece*, 151–67.

Map of Greece

1832 London Convention

Frontiers today

solely to those who fought and suffered. But no less significant an achievement on the part of the Greek leadership was to mobilise support from abroad—first from volunteers such as Lord Byron, and latterly from the governments of Great Britain, France and Russia.

It is a fitting tribute to that fact, that on 25 March 2021, in spite of a third wave of the Covid-19 pandemic rampant throughout much of Europe, including Greece, the present-day governments of those countries were represented at a commemorative parade in the centre of Athens by HRH the Prince of Wales, the defence minister of France and the prime minister of the Russian Federation.

EPILOGUE

The true significance of the events taking place around them was perhaps most accurately, if necessarily imprecisely, divined by those British poets who stand out among the philhellenic movement, Shelley and Byron. In a passage deleted by his publisher from the Preface to *Hellas*, written in the autumn of 1821, that remained unpublished until 1892, Shelley wrote:

> This is the age of the war of the oppressed against the oppressors [... . A] new race has arisen throughout Europe, nursed in the abhorrence of the opinions which are its chains, and she will continue to produce fresh generations to accomplish that destiny which tyrants foresee and dread.[33]

---

[33] Shelley, 'Preface' to *Hellas*, 448 and editor's note.

And Byron, in conversations recorded during the three short months that he spent at Missolonghi before his death, also prophetically identified in the Revolution in Greece a turning point in the affairs of Europe. What was being achieved by the Greek revolutionaries, Byron foresaw, was to create an entirely new kind of political state, one that in future would be emulated throughout the continent:

> those principles which are now in action in Greece will gradually produce their effect, both here *and in other countries*[.] [...] I cannot [...] calculate to what a height Greece may rise. Hitherto it has been a subject for the hymns and elegies of fanatics and enthusiasts; but now it will draw the attention of the politician.[34]

Shelley's radicalism was more idealistic than based on practical politics; Byron had the shrewder grasp of what could possibly be achieved. But both, near the end of their short lives, were looking far into the future. And what they saw has indeed, in ways that neither of them

---

[34] Pietro Gamba, *A Narrative of Lord Byron's Last Journey to Greece* (London: John Murray, 1825), 121 (emphasis added), 212.

could ever have imagined, come to pass. Greece and the Greeks were indeed the first—the pioneers, the advance guard, if you like—to tread a path that in 1830 had never yet been followed to a successful conclusion in the Old World of Europe. Since then, their example has been followed by just about every modern European state, and many more all over the world.

FURTHER READING

Brewer, David, *The Flame of Freedom: The Greek War of Independence, 1821–1833* (London: John Murray, 2001).

Mazower, Mark, *The Greek Revolution: 1821 and the Making of Modern Europe* (London: Allen Lane, 2021).

Kitromilides, Paschalis and Constantinos Tsoukalas (eds), *The Greek Revolution: A Critical Dictionary* (Cambridge, MA: Harvard University Press, 2021).

Pizanias, Petros (ed.), *The Greek Revolution of 1821: A European Event* (Istanbul: Isis, 2011; Greek original published 2009).

St Clair, William, *That Greece Might Still Be Free: The Philhellenes in the War of Independence* (London: Open Book, 2008; first published 1972).

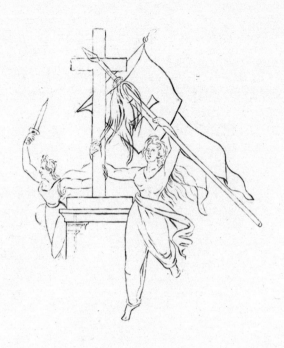

READ THE
MODERN GREEK CLASSICS

The Modern Greek Classics series highlights
the most significant writers, poets, and works
of literature of the nineteenth and twentieth
centuries in English translation. A tour of
Greece through its literary history.

www.aiorabooks.com